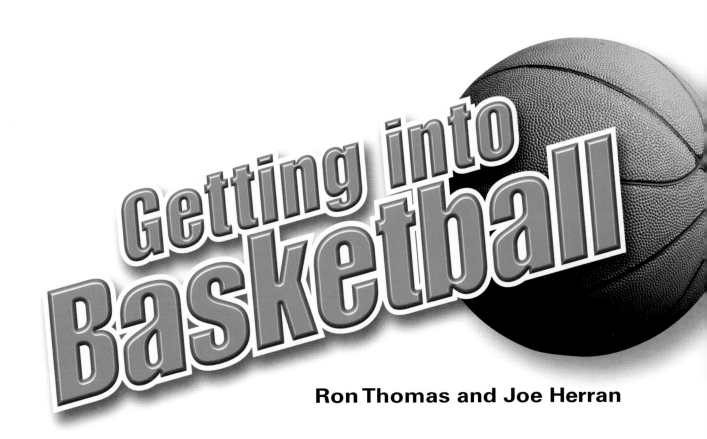

Getting into Basketball

Ron Thomas and Joe Herran

CHELSEA HOUSE
PUBLISHERS
A Haights Cross Communications Company ®
Philadelphia

This edition first published in 2006 in the United States of America by Chelsea House Publishers, a subsidiary of Haights Cross Communications.

A Haights Cross Communications ⭐ Company ®

Chelsea House Publishers
2080 Cabot Boulevard West, Suite 201
Langhorne, PA 19047-1813

The Chelsea House world wide web address is www.chelseahouse.com

First published in 2005 by
MACMILLAN EDUCATION AUSTRALIA PTY LTD
627 Chapel Street, South Yarra 3141

Visit our website at www.macmillan.com.au

Associated companies and representatives throughout the world.

Library of Congress Cataloguing-in-Publication Data Applied for.
ISBN 0 7910 8809 X

Edited by Helena Newton
Text and cover design by Cristina Neri, Canary Graphic Design
Illustrations by Nives Porcellato and Andy Craig
Photo research by Legend Images

Printed in China

Acknowledgments
The authors wish to acknowledge and thank Mary McGregor for her assistance and advice in the writing of this book.

The authors and the publisher are grateful to the following for permission to reproduce copyright material:

Cover photographs: Basketball courtesy of Photodisc, and player courtesy of Corbis Digital Stock.

Australian Picture Library, pp. 7 (bottom), 9 (bottom), 26, 27; Corbis Digital Stock, pp. 5, 9 top;
D. Clarke Evans/NBAE/Getty Images, p. 22; Jonathan Daniel/Getty Images, p. 24; Stephen Dunn/Getty Images, p. 21; Andy Hayt/NBAE/Getty Images, p. 4; Mitchell Layton/NBAE/Getty Images, pp. 7 (top), 23; Catherine Steenkeste/NBAE/Getty Images, p. 29; Photodisc, pp. 1, 11 (background); Picture Media/ REUTERS/Mike Blake, p. 28; Picture Media/ REUTERS/David Gray, p. 30 (right); Picture Media/ REUTERS/Adrees Latif, p. 30 (left).

Contents

Glossary words

When a word is printed in **bold**, you can look up its meaning in the Glossary on page 31.

The game

Basketball is a fast game requiring stamina, agility, speed, and good hand-to-eye coordination. It is played by more than 400 million people in countries all over the world. Competitions for amateurs take place at local, state, and national levels. Many countries have their own basketball federation, which runs the sport in that country. At the international level, the Fédération Internationale de Basketball (FIBA) is the governing body that sets the rules for international events, including Olympic competition.

Did you know?

The biggest basketball league, with 27 professional teams, is the National Basketball Association (NBA) in the United States.

Shaquille O'Neal of the Los Angeles Lakers and Rasheed Wallace of the Detroit Pistons playing in an NBA final in Los Angeles, California

The history of basketball

Basketball was created in 1891 by a Canadian-born American physical education teacher, Dr. James A. Naismith. He invented the indoor game of basketball to keep his student football players fit during the winter. Naismith attached a wicker basket to the balcony at each end of a gymnasium. The students were divided into teams of nine and they played their first basketball game using a soccer ball.

Playing a match

The aim of the two teams playing a basketball match is to score more points than the opposing team. Points are scored by throwing the ball through a basket suspended from a ring and backboard. Each team can have 10 players but only five players from each team can be on the court at any time. The remaining players are used as **substitutes** at different times during the game.

The aim of a basketball game is to score more points than the opposing team by throwing the ball through the basket.

The game starts with a **jump ball**. A player from each team stands on either side of the center line and the referee throws the ball into the air. The players leap up and try to tap the ball to a teammate. The players then move the ball up and down the court by **passing** the ball to teammates or **dribbling** it toward their basket. The team with the most points at the end of the game wins.

Referees control the game, making sure that players obey the rules. Breaking a rule is called a **foul**. If a player commits a foul, play stops and the ball is given to the opposing team. Players who foul repeatedly during a game can be sent off the court.

A basketball match is played in four 12-minute quarters or in two 20-minute halves.

Equipment

The only equipment needed for a fun game is a ball and a basket. At competition level, however, equipment must meet standards set by the sport's governing body.

Basketball

A basketball is a round ball made of real or artificial orange leather. It measures 29.5 to 30.7 inches (75 to 78 centimeters) around and weighs 20 to 23 ounces (567 to 650 grams). Inside the ball is a rubber bladder that is pumped up to inflate it.

Backboards and baskets

Backboards are made of special safety glass that will not break. Other materials, such as **perspex** and wood, are also used. Backboards are 3.9 feet (1.2 meters) from the baseline, or the end of the playing area.

Baskets have two parts: a steel ring and a net. The ring is at least 17.7 inches (45 centimeters) across and is attached 5.9 inches (15 centimeters) in front of the backboard and 10 feet (3.05 meters) from the floor. A rectangle is painted onto the backboard, centered behind the ring. The net is attached to the ring in 12 places.

A basketball backboard

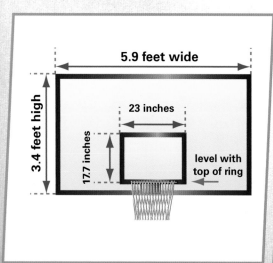

Top view of ring and backboard

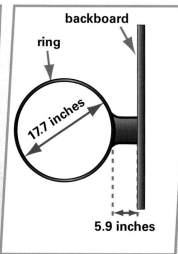

Side view of net, ring, and backboard

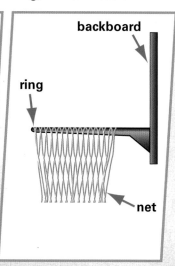

Clothing

Men and women basketballers wear similar clothing that is usually loose-fitting for comfort and easy movement. A player's number must be displayed on the front and the back of the uniform shirt, called a singlet.

Shoes and socks

Shoes come in many styles and colors. Some players wear low-cut shoes while others choose high-cut shoes. High-cut shoes support the ankles. Soles should be made of rubber for a good grip on the court. Cotton socks absorb sweat and keep a player's feet comfortable.

Singlet and shorts

A singlet and long shorts are light and comfortable for a game that is generally played indoors.

Protective clothing

Protective knee and elbow pads can be worn by beginning and younger players to cushion falls. A mouthguard protects a player's teeth and gums.

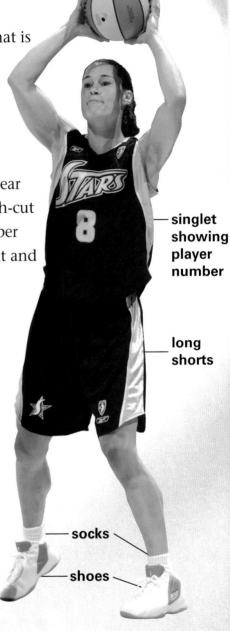

singlet showing player number

long shorts

socks

shoes

Rule

Players must not wear jewelry on any part of their bodies.

Even experienced players wear protective clothing.

The court

Basketball is played on a rectangular court. Indoor courts are usually polished wood while outdoor courts are usually made of asphalt. The backboards and baskets are at either end of the court.

A basketball court

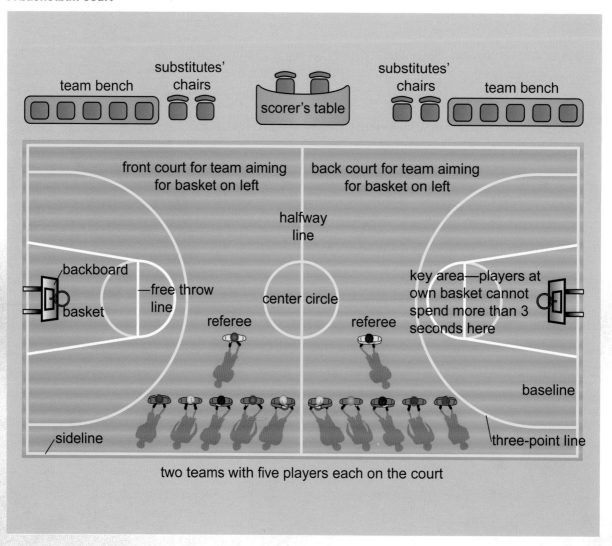

team bench

substitutes' chairs

scorer's table

substitutes' chairs

team bench

front court for team aiming for basket on left

back court for team aiming for basket on left

halfway line

backboard

free throw line

center circle

key area—players at own basket cannot spend more than 3 seconds here

basket

referee

referee

baseline

sideline

three-point line

two teams with five players each on the court

The players

During a game, all team members play **offense**, when they are controlling the ball or attacking, and **defense**, when they are blocking the play of the opposition.

In the correct defensive stance, the player is bent low with arms outstretched to prevent an opponent from dribbling.

Offensive players

Offensive players aim to score as many points as possible. Good offensive players always:

- shoot if there is a good chance of making the shot
- shoot when their teammates are in position for a **rebound**
- spread out to give the shooter space and to try to confuse the defensive players
- pass quickly to teammates.

Defensive players

Defensive players aim to keep the opposing team from scoring. Good defensive players always:

- place themselves between an opponent and the basket he or she is aiming for
- use the correct defensive stance
- watch the opponent's waist to avoid being misled by **faking**. The direction of a player's hips indicates the way the player will run.

A defensive player stands with knees bent and one arm raised to defend against a lone offensive player.

Skills

Beginning players learn the basic skills of basketball, which include learning the correct stance, how to perform a jump ball, dribbling, passing, shooting for goal, faking, rebounding, and playing defense. With practice, players will develop these skills and improve their performance.

Basic stance

A player in basic stance

The basketball player in basic stance:

- has the feet shoulder-width apart with one foot slightly ahead of the other
- keeps the knees bent or slightly flexed
- distributes weight evenly on both feet
- stands on the balls of the feet
- keeps the back straight and leans slightly forward
- keeps the hands up and ready
- looks forward with the head up.

From the correct stance, the basketball player can:

- accelerate to full speed in just a few steps
- move quickly toward the ball to receive a pass
- make a strong move away from a defender
- jump for a rebound after a missed shot
- slide or shuffle sideways to defend against an opposition player
- leap into the air for a quick jump shot
- dribble past a defender.

A player on the move

Rule
A player who loses balance, falls on the court, and fouls an opposing player is penalized and the ball is given to the opposing team.

Jump ball

In the jump ball, two opposing players jump for a ball that a referee has tossed above and between them. The players try to tap the ball to their teammates to gain possession of the ball. The jump ball is used:

- at the start of the game and at the start of all other periods, also called the **tip-off**
- for all overtime periods.

The rules of the jump ball are:

- when the referee throws the ball into the air, the ball cannot be touched until it has reached its highest point
- if the ball hits the ground before either player touches it, the referee will throw the ball up again.

Players involved in a jump ball keep their eyes on the ball and jump at full stretch to try to knock the ball to a teammate.

Dribbling

Dribbling is bouncing the ball with one hand while moving forward. To control the ball while dribbling, the player spreads the fingers as wide as possible and bounces the ball with the fingertips. The player avoids hitting or slapping the ball and keeps it below waist height. Bouncing the ball too high when dribbling may cause the referee to call "carrying the ball" and the ball will be given to the other team. While dribbling, the player watches for opportunities to pass the ball to a teammate and for threatening opponents.

Crossover dribble

The crossover dribble is used to change direction and to get past a defender. During the crossover dribble, the offensive player dribbles the ball from one hand to the other.

The crossover dribble

Between-the-legs dribble

The offensive player also changes direction during the between-the-legs dribble. The player dribbles the ball between his or her own legs, swapping the ball from one hand to the other while turning away from a defender.

The between-the-legs dribble

Reverse dribble

For the reverse dribble, the player changes dribbling hands and, at the same time, pivots to turn his or her back to an opponent. Taking a long step, the player passes the opponent.

The reverse dribble

Behind-the-back dribble

During the behind-the-back dribble, the player dribbles the ball out to one side and moves it behind the back. Then, by pushing the top and rear of the ball, it is bounced to the other side of the body.

The behind-the-back dribble

Rules

A player moving down the court must always dribble the ball. Walking, running, or moving both feet without dribbling the ball is called **traveling** *and results in the ball being given to the opposition.*

Players cannot dribble, stop, and then start dribbling again unless an opposing player has touched the ball.

Passing

Passing is the quickest way to move a ball up and down the court. A good pass is accurate, well-timed, and at the correct speed. The receiver of a pass should not have to stretch or strain to catch the ball. The pass needs to be fast but not so fast that the receiver might not be able to control it.

Chest pass

To make a chest pass, the player holds the ball in front of the lower half of the chest, with elbows tucked in. The thumbs are behind the ball and fingers are spread out on the sides of the ball. With the knees slightly bent, the player leans the head and shoulders toward the target. The player steps toward the target, extending the arms to push the ball away with the wrists, thumbs, and fingers. The player follows through and completes the pass with thumbs pointing to the floor.

Rule

If a pass is missed by a team member and the ball goes out of bounds, the ball is given to the opposing team.

A chest pass

1 The player holds the ball close to the chest.

2 If possible, the player takes a step toward the person to whom he or she is passing.

3 The player pushes the ball away to complete the pass.

Bounce pass

To make a bounce pass, the player pushes the ball away with wrists and fingers at waist height while crouching slightly and leaning forward. The ball is bounced to a teammate and should strike the court only once before reaching the teammate. The ball should not bounce higher than hip height. At the end of the pass, the player's thumbs and palms face the floor.

The bounce pass

One-handed or baseball pass

For the one-handed or baseball pass, the player begins by holding the ball in front of the chest with both hands. The player drops one hand to hold the ball in the other hand above shoulder height and a little to the side with the elbow tucked in. The player steps forward onto the foot opposite to the hand holding the ball. Using the wrist, the ball is flicked forward.

The one-handed or baseball pass

Overhead pass

For the two-handed overhead pass, the player holds the ball with both hands directly above the head. The thumbs are behind the ball and the fingers are spread around the sides. The player takes a step forward and releases the ball by flicking the wrists. When the pass is completed, the fingers and palms face the floor.

An overhead pass

1

2

Shooting for goal

The aim of passing, catching, and dribbling the ball is to set up a teammate with an opportunity to score points by putting the ball in the basket. When shooting for goal, the player's fingertips control the ball and the snap of the wrists propels the ball into the basket. Players score with a variety of shots.

Layup

The layup is a basic one-handed shot for goal made on the run. The player approaches the basket on an angle from either left or right. From a position as close as possible to the basket, the player jumps high from one foot, lifting the ball, which is held with both hands. Once the player is as high as possible in the air and at full stretch, the supporting hand is lowered and the ball is banked (thrown and bounced lightly) off the backboard and into the basket with the other hand. Players need to learn to approach the basket from the left and the right and to layup with either hand.

The player runs as close as possible to the basket and makes a layup with one hand.

Reverse layup

For the reverse layup, the player approaches the basket in the same way as for a layup. But when the player finds that an opponent is too close or in a position to block the shot, the player continues to move underneath the basket. With his or her back to the basket, the player jumps high and banks the ball softly off the backboard with one hand.

Sometimes the player may not be in the correct position to bank the ball off the backboard. In this case, the player shoots the ball straight up and spins it into the basket without hitting the backboard.

SKILLS

The reverse layup

Set shot

For the set shot, the player holds the ball in both hands and faces the basket. The feet are shoulder-width apart and one foot is slightly forward. The shooting hand is underneath and behind the ball and the other hand supports the side of the ball. The player's knees are bent as the ball is raised just above the head. The guiding hand is taken off the ball and the arms and legs are fully straightened. The wrist snaps as the ball is released. A player given a free shot due to a foul by an opposing player usually uses the set shot.

The player's feet remain on the floor during the set shot.

Jump shot

The player prepares for the jump shot in the same way as for a set shot. When making the shot, the player jumps off the ground evenly and straight up, bringing the ball level with the forehead. At the peak of the jump, the guiding hand is taken off the ball, the arms are straightened fully and the wrist snaps as the ball is released.

A jump shot is made over the heads of the defense and often from a long way out from the basket.

Dunk shot

For the **dunk** shot, the player dribbles the ball close to the basket and springs up, holding the ball in one or both hands. When the ball and the player's wrists are above the basket, the wrists snap down to push the ball down or dunk it into the basket.

The "slam dunk" is one of the most spectacular shots in basketball.

Hook shot

To make the hook shot, the player dribbles the ball while looking at the basket. For a right-hand hook, the player holds the basketball in the right hand, pushes off with the left leg, and lifts the right knee high into the air. The player snaps the right wrist and arcs the ball overhead and into the basket.

The hook shot

▼Rule

Once a team has control of the ball, the players have a set amount of time to shoot. The time allowed depends on the rules of the competition. If the ball is not shot within the time limit, the ball goes to the opposing team.

Faking

Faking is a movement to try to throw an opponent off-guard. The player with the ball moves quickly in one direction but then switches direction to confuse the opponent. The defensive player watches the opponent's waist. The direction in which the hips are facing is the direction in which the player will run.

Faking

1 The player begins moving in one direction.

2 The player quickly switches direction and moves past the opponent.

Faking after a dribble

To fake after a dribble, the player acts as if he or she wants to pass the ball in one direction but then stops abruptly and throws it in the other direction.

Faking when going for a shot

To fake when going for a shot, the player with the ball bobs or jerks the head and shoulders in one direction. When the defender moves in that direction, the player moves to the other side and shoots.

The pivot

When the player stops dribbling or has received the ball, he or she must not move both feet. The player must decide which foot is the pivot foot and that foot must not leave the ground while the player continues to hold the ball. The player may turn in any direction by lifting the other foot. If the pivot foot is lifted, the ball is given to the opposing team.

Rebounding

Rebounding is the name given to the jump made to gain possession of the ball after it has bounced off the backboard or the ring.

Defensive rebound

The defensive player is usually closer to the basket than the player who shot for goal. To take the defensive rebound, the defensive player tries to stand between the opponent and the basket. This is called "blocking" or "blocking out." The defender takes a rebound with both hands and either dribbles down the court or passes quickly to a teammate.

The defensive rebound is used to stop the opponents from getting the ball back after they have taken a shot at the basket.

Offensive rebound

It is much more difficult for an offensive player to take a rebound because the defensive player is usually closer to the basket and in a better position to get a missed shot. When the offensive player sees that a shot is going to miss, he or she quickly finds a position closer to the basket than the defensive player to take the offensive rebound.

The offensive player must time the jump carefully to try to catch the ball at the height of the jump.

Rules

Basketball rules for all international competitions are formulated by the Fédération Internationale de Basketball (FIBA). Players need to learn and understand the basic rules before they are ready to play basketball.

Fouls

There are two kinds of fouls: personal fouls and technical fouls.

Personal foul

A personal foul is called when the player:

- holds, pushes, grips, or trips another player
- blocks an opponent by extending an arm, shoulder, hip, or knee, or by using rough tactics
- charges into an opponent.

A personal foul is called when the player makes contact with an opponent, whether the ball is in play or not. When the player is called for a foul, the player must raise a hand to show he or she is the player the foul has been called against. The referee signals the reason for the foul and the player's number to the scorer. The opposing player is given a sideline throw-in or, if the player missed shooting a goal because of the foul, two free shots at goal.

A referee uses a signal to call a foul against a player.

Technical foul

A technical foul is called when the player ignores official warnings and is showing bad sportsmanship. Coaches and substitute players can also be called for technical fouls. Technical fouls are called for unsportsmanlike behavior, such as:

- arguing or insulting another player
- wasting time and delaying the game
- using bad language
- talking disrespectfully to the officials.

When a technical foul is called, the opposing team gets one free throw and is given control of the ball at center court. A player or coach who receives two technical fouls in a game is sent out of the arena.

Out of bounds

A ball is out out of bounds when:

- it touches a player who is out of the playing court or standing on any of the lines marking the outside of the court
- it touches the floor outside of the court. When this happens, possession of the ball is given against the team that last touched the ball.

Rule

Any player who receives five fouls during a game can no longer play and must be replaced for the remainder of the game. In some professional codes of basketball, such as the National Basketball Association (NBA), the number of fouls is six before ejection.

When a technical foul is called, a player on the opposing team can take a free shot.

Scoring and timing

A goal can count for two or three points depending on which area of the court it is thrown from. A goal from the free throw line counts for one point. FIBA rules state that a game is played in two 20-minute halves with a 10- or 15-minute interval between them. If a game is tied, then an overtime period is played.

Scorer and assistant scorer

The scorer's role includes:

● recording names and numbers of players and substitutes
● keeping a record of all points scored
● recording the number of free throws attempted
● recording personal and technical fouls against players
● recording any technical fouls charged against coaches.

The assistant scorer operates the scoreboard and assists the scorer.

Timekeeper and 24-second-clock operator

In some competitions, officials watch an instant replay to help them make a decision.

The timekeeper keeps a record of playing and stopping times using a game clock and a stopwatch, and sounds a signal for time-out periods and the end of play.

A team that gains possession of the ball has 24 seconds to shoot for goal. The 24-second-clock operator checks that a shot for goal is made within the time limit. In Olympic competitions, the time limit is 30 seconds.

Referees

There are two referees for a game of basketball. The referees are responsible for controlling the game and calling fouls when players break the rules. The referees show the scorer which foul has been called using a series of hand signals. Referees also use signals to indicate which players have scored a goal and whether they have scored a one-, two-, or three-point goal.

These are some of the signals used by basketball referees.

Chopping one hand with the other hand or finger signals time-in.

Waving the wrist while holding up fingers signals the number of points given.

Forming a T shape with hands signals a technical foul.

Thumbs up signals a jump ball.

Raising a clenched fist signals a personal foul.

Rotating fists signals traveling.

Moving arms across body signals that score and play are canceled.

Imitating a push signals pushing.

Hands on hips signals blocking.

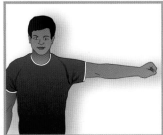

Clenched fist extended to one side signals charging.

Holding up a number of fingers signals that the player with that number has offended.

Gripping one wrist signals holding.

Player fitness

Basketballers need to be fit if they are to perform to the best of their ability. Running, swimming, and cycling build stamina and fitness.

Warming up and stretching

Before a game or a practice session, it is important for players to warm up all their muscles. This helps prevent injuries, such as muscle tears, strains, and joint injuries. A gentle jog of five or six laps around the basketball court will help players warm up. Stretching makes players more flexible and helps the muscles and joints move easily on the court.

Players warm up and stretch before a basketball game to prevent injuries.

Neck stretches

The player tilts the head forward and slowly rolls the head to one shoulder and then the other. These exercises help prevent stiffness in the neck and keep the neck flexible.

Side stretches

The player raises the right hand above the head and slowly leans to the left. Then the stretch is repeated, raising the left hand above the head and leaning slowly to the right.

Calf stretches

The player places one foot in front of the other and leans forward, but keeps the back heel on the ground. The player pushes forward until the calf muscle in the back leg stretches. The stretch is repeated for the other leg.

Thigh stretches

Standing on one leg, the player holds the ankle of the raised leg. The player pulls the foot back to stretch the thigh, keeping the knees close together. The player can lean against a wall or hold onto another player for balance. The stretch is then repeated for the other leg.

Back stretch

The player crouches down on all fours with the head up and back flat. Then the player tucks the head under and arches the back upward. The player feels the stretch in the upper back.

Groin stretch

The player sits on the floor with the knees bent and pointing out to either side. Holding onto the ankles, the player pulls them gently in toward the body. The player pushes down gently on the thighs with the arms so that the legs move toward the floor.

Hamstring stretch

The player sits on the floor with the legs extended in front of the body and the knees straight. Bending forward slowly, the player reaches toward the toes.

Stretching exercises, such as the hamstring stretch, are done in an easy and relaxed way, and each position is held for at least 10 seconds.

Competition

The Fédération Internationale de Basketball (FIBA) is the world governing body for basketball. It is an association of 212 national basketball federations from countries around the world. FIBA was founded in Geneva, Switzerland, in 1932. FIBA's headquarters were in Munich, Germany, for many years before returning to Geneva in 2002. FIBA is recognized as the authority for basketball by the International Olympic Committee (IOC).

FIBA's role is to:

- set the official basketball rules, the specifications for equipment and facilities, and all other regulations for international and Olympic competitions
- appoint all international referees
- regulate the transfer of players from one country to another
- control all international competitions.

World Championship

FIBA organizes World Championship tournaments for men and women basketballers every four years.

The winner of the Men's World Championship title in 2002 was Yugoslavia.

Professional basketball leagues

There are a number of professional basketball leagues for both men and women in the United States, Europe, Asia, and Australia. The biggest and most famous are the National Basketball Association (NBA) and the Women's National Basketball Association (WNBA) in the United States.

Professional women's basketball competitions in the United States are run by the WNBA.

The NBA has teams representing cities in both the United States and Canada, and these teams include players from all over the world. The NBA season is played from November until April.

The WNBA was formed in 1997 and has teams representing cities in the United States. Top female players from around the world are part of the teams. The WNBA season is played from April until September.

Both the NBA and the WNBA have some rules that are slightly different from the FIBA rules. For example, an NBA game is played in four 12-minute quarters, rather than in two 20-minute halves.

> **Did you know?**
>
> *The first NBA Championship was played in 1947 between the Philadelphia Warriors and the Chicago Stags. The Warriors won the series 4–1.*

Olympic basketball

The United States and Korean women's basketball teams competing during the 2004 Olympic Games in Athens

An Olympic basketball game consists of two 20-minute halves. A team must shoot for goal within 30 seconds of gaining possession of the ball or it is given to the opposition.

In both men's and women's basketball, a preliminary tournament is held and nine teams win their way into the Olympic competition. Three other teams have an automatic place in the competition. They are the first and second place finishers from the previous Olympics and the team of the host country. The 12 finalists are divided into two groups of six, and each country plays the other five teams in their group. The top four from each group go to the quarterfinals. The four winners of the quarterfinals play the semifinals. The two countries that win the semifinals play for the gold and silver medals. The two countries that lose the semifinals play for the bronze.

Did you know?

Basketball became an Olympic sport for men at the Berlin Games in 1936. It was played on an outdoor tennis stadium on courts of sand and clay. Women's basketball became an Olympic event at the Montreal Games in 1976.

The Australian and Japanese men's teams competing during the Paralympic basketball tournament in Sydney 2000

Glossary

defense	when a team does not have possession of the ball and is trying to block the play of the team that does
dribbling	when a player repeatedly pushes, pats, taps, or bats the ball toward the floor with one hand, causing it to bounce back up to either hand
dunk	a one- or two-handed shot in which the player jumps and firmly pushes the ball down into the basket
faking	a deceptive move to throw a defender off balance and allow an offensive player to shoot or receive a pass
foul	an action by a player or coach that breaks the rules
jump ball	when a referee tosses a ball above and between two opposing players who jump for the ball and try to tap it to their teammates to gain possession; used to start the game, all overtime periods, and sometimes to restart play
offense	when a team has possession of the ball
passing	throwing or bouncing the ball to a teammate
perspex	a clear plastic
rebound	when a player jumps to catch the ball after it has bounced off the ring or the backboard following an unsuccessful shot
substitutes	players who wait beside the court and are sent in to play when other players leave the court
tip-off	the beginning of a basketball game or the start of another period such as a half or quarter
traveling	taking a step or running with the ball before dribbling, also called walking

Index